TRICERATOPS

BY REBECCA SABELKO

EPIC

BELLWETHER MEDIA • MINNEAPOLIS, MN

EPIC BOOKS are no ordinary books. They burst with intense action, high-speed heroics, and shadows of the unknown. Are you ready for an Epic adventure?

This edition first published in 2020 by Bellwether Media, Inc.

No part of this publication may be reproduced in whole or in part without written permission of the publisher. For information regarding permission, write to Bellwether Media, Inc., Attention: Permissions Department, 6012 Blue Circle Drive, Minnetonka, MN 55343.

Library of Congress Cataloging-in-Publication Data

Names: Sabelko, Rebecca, author.
Title: Triceratops / by Rebecca Sabelko.
Description: Minneapolis, MN : Bellwether Media, Inc., [2020] | Series: Epic. The World of Dinosaurs |
Audience: Ages 7-12. | Audience: Grades 2 to 7. | Includes bibliographical references and index.
Identifiers: LCCN 2019002826 (print) | LCCN 2019005223 (ebook) |
  ISBN 9781618916617 (ebook) | ISBN 9781644870891 (hardcover : alk. paper) |
  ISBN 9781618917362 (pbk. : alk. paper)
Subjects: LCSH: Triceratops--Juvenile literature. |
  Paleontology--Cretaceous--Juvenile literature. | CYAC: Dinosaurs.
Classification: LCC QE862.O65 (ebook) | LCC QE862.O65 S2445 2020 (print) | DDC 567.915/8--dc23
LC record available at https://lccn.loc.gov/2019002826

Editor: Betsy Rathburn   Designer: Jeffrey Kollock

Printed in the United States of America, North Mankato, MN

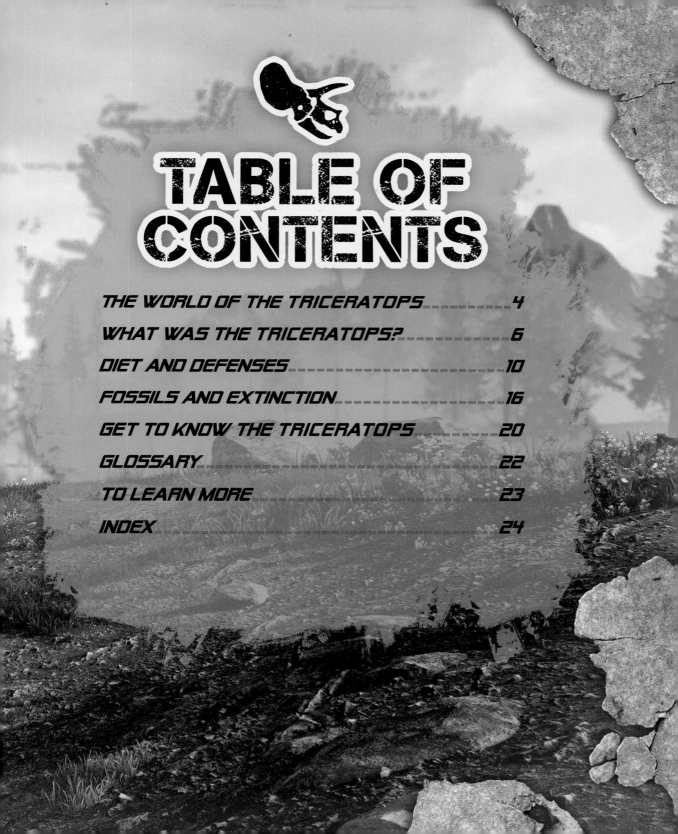

TABLE OF CONTENTS

THE WORLD OF THE TRICERATOPS

frill

PRONUNCIATION

try-SAIR-uh-TOPS

NAME GAME

Triceratops means "three-horned face."

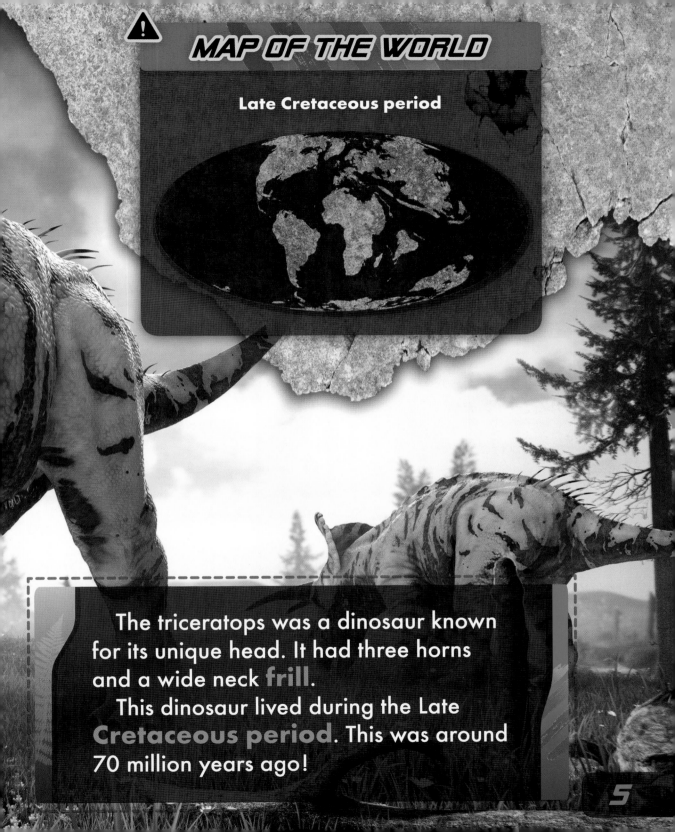

Late Cretaceous period

The triceratops was a dinosaur known for its unique head. It had three horns and a wide neck **frill**.

This dinosaur lived during the Late **Cretaceous period**. This was around 70 million years ago!

WHAT WAS THE TRICERATOPS?

The triceratops was huge! It weighed up to 16,000 pounds (7,257 kilograms).

A giant head made up one-third of the dinosaur's body length. Its frill was 3 feet (1 meter) wide!

15 feet (5 meters)

10 feet (3 meters)

5 feet (2 meters)

The frill was likely used to show off to **mates**. It may have also helped the dinosaur cool off on hot days.

⚠️ **LONG HORNS**

Some triceratops horns were more than 3 feet (1 meter) long!

The triceratops used its horns to stay safe. They helped fight off other dinosaurs and claim **territory**.

DIET AND DEFENSES

TEETH HELP

Triceratops teeth worked like scissors. This made it easier to chew hard plants.

This dinosaur ate a lot of food! Many strong plants grew where the triceratops lived. These plants were hard to eat.

The triceratops used its strong beak to snap tough plants.

TRICERATOPS DIET

ferns

shrubs

leafy plants

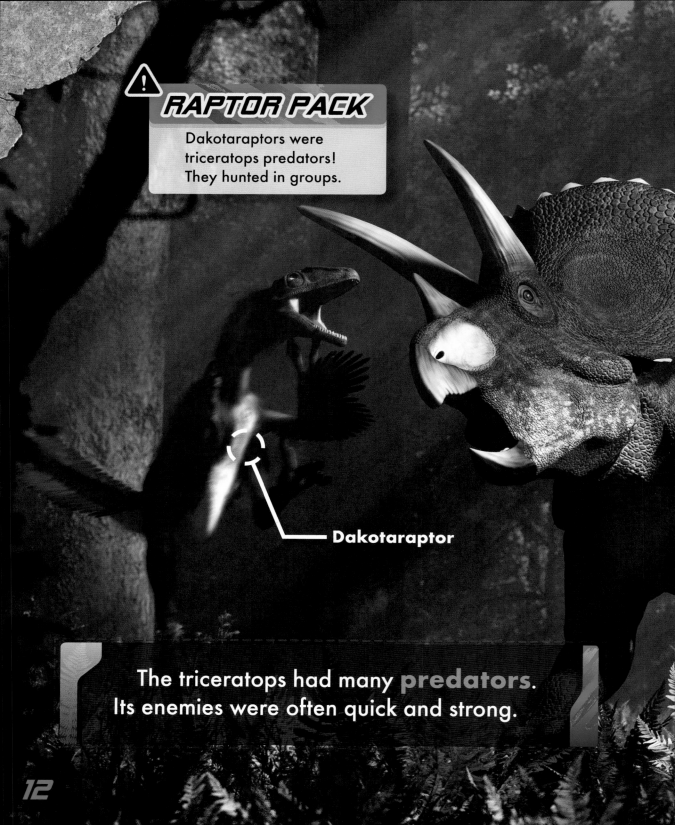

⚠️ **RAPTOR PACK**

Dakotaraptors were triceratops predators! They hunted in groups.

Dakotaraptor

The triceratops had many **predators**. Its enemies were often quick and strong.

The triceratops could not outrun enemies. Its body was too heavy. The dinosaur had to stand its ground!

Scientists believe the triceratops tried to look big and strong. It flashed its frill and horns.

BIG BITE!

Scientists have found triceratops frills with large bite marks. The marks fit Tyrannosaurus rex teeth!

The triceratops charged at predators. Its sharp horns drove enemies away!

FOSSILS AND EXTINCTION

Scientists believe a large **meteorite** hit Earth around 66 million years ago. The changing **climate** caused fewer plants to grow. The triceratops could not find enough food. These changes lead to a **mass extinction**.

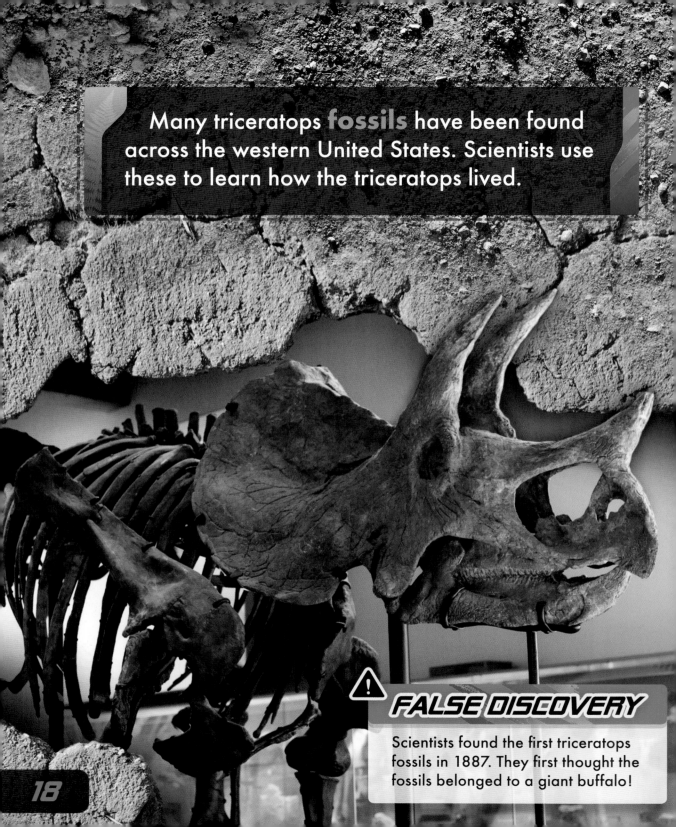

Many triceratops **fossils** have been found across the western United States. Scientists use these to learn how the triceratops lived.

⚠️ **FALSE DISCOVERY**

Scientists found the first triceratops fossils in 1887. They first thought the fossils belonged to a giant buffalo!

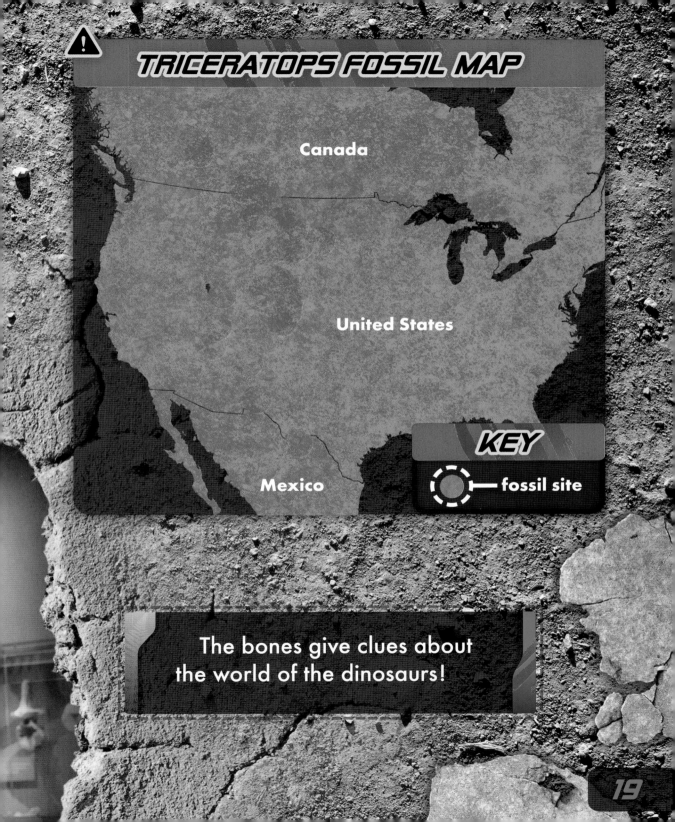

TRICERATOPS FOSSIL MAP

Canada

United States

Mexico

KEY

fossil site

The bones give clues about
the world of the dinosaurs!

GET TO KNOW THE TRICERATOPS

frill

horns

beak

HEIGHT up to 10 feet (3 meters) tall

WEIGHT up to 16,000 pounds (7,257 kilograms)

LENGTH up to 30 feet (9 meters) long

⚠️ **ERA**

100 million to 66 million years ago during the Late Cretaceous period

Triassic | Jurassic | Cretaceous

⚠️ **FIRST FOSSILS FOUND**

1887 in Wyoming

⚠️ **FOOD**

ferns **leafy plants**

⚠️ **LOCATION**

North America

⚠️ **FOUND BY**

George Cannon

GLOSSARY

climate—the usual weather in a certain area over long periods of time

Cretaceous period—the last period of the Mesozoic era that happened between 145 million to 66 million years ago; the Late Cretaceous period began around 100 million years ago.

fossils—the remains of living things that lived long ago

frill—a bony fan at the back of a triceratops's head

mass extinction—an event that causes plants and animals to die out completely

mates—pairs of adult animals that produce babies

meteorite—a space rock that hits Earth

predators—animals that hunt other animals for food

territory—the land area where an animal lives

TO LEARN MORE

AT THE LIBRARY

Allatson, Amy. *Triceratops*. New York, N.Y.: KidHaven Publishing, 2018.

Gilbert, Sara. *Triceratops*. Mankato, Minn.: Creative Education, 2019.

Waxman, Laura Hamilton. *Discovering Triceratops*. Mankato, Minn.: Amicus, 2019.

ON THE WEB

FACTSURFER

Factsurfer.com gives you a safe, fun way to find more information.

1. Go to www.factsurfer.com.

2. Enter "triceratops" into the search box and click 🔍 .

3. Select your book cover to see a list of related web sites.

INDEX